THE ROLE OF
BRITISH STRATEGY
IN THE
GREAT WAR

The Role of
British Strategy
in the
Great War

BY

C. R. M. F. CRUTTWELL, M.A.
Principal of Hertford College, Oxford

CAMBRIDGE
AT THE UNIVERSITY PRESS
1936

CAMBRIDGE UNIVERSITY PRESS
Cambridge, New York, Melbourne, Madrid, Cape Town,
Singapore, São Paulo, Delhi, Tokyo, Mexico City

Cambridge University Press
The Edinburgh Building, Cambridge CB2 8RU, UK

Published in the United States of America by Cambridge University Press, New York

www.cambridge.org
Information on this title: www.cambridge.org/9781107605206

First published 1936
First paperback edition 2011

A catalogue record for this publication is available from the British Library

ISBN 978-1-107-60520-6 Paperback

CONTENTS

PREFACE

This little book contains the substance of lectures delivered in 1936 for the Lees-Knowles Foundation, at Trinity College, Cambridge. I am indebted to the Master and Fellows of that College for their invitation and to the Syndics of the University Press for suggesting the publication of these lectures.

C. R. M. F. C.

HERTFORD COLLEGE
OXFORD
March 1936

Chapter I

THE BRITISH TRADITION IN
CONTINENTAL COALITIONS

I

THE GREAT WAR, except for its unexampled magnitude, was a type with
which British statesmen and soldiers were
traditionally familiar. Once every century since
the end of the sixteenth we had been engaged in
a struggle to uphold what was idealistically called
the freedom of Europe and more prosaically the
balance of power. In each case England was
directly touched by the spur of self-preservation,
by the danger of a naval rivalry more or less intense, and by the threat of hostile dominion in the
most precious outwork of her security, the Low
Countries. In each case too she occupied within
her membership of loose and often jarring continental coalitions a peculiar, indeed a unique,
position. Her territory was never violated, her
command of the sea gave an almost embarrassing
choice of objectives for her campaigns, and a

semi-detached eclectic method of waging war. England in the past had never been the direct military instrument of the overthrow of the over-mastering power against which the coalition was arranged. She had been the inspirer and the reviver of such coalitions, she had been consistently "the good milch cow" from which its members sucked subsidies inexhaustible in repute; she had in fact the tradition of waging continental war with the most lavish expenditure in money, and the greatest economy in human life. In the Napoleonic War, apart from the sums raised by taxation, some five hundred million pounds were added to the National Debt; but our loss of life scarcely exceeded 100,000 men or about an eighteenth of that of the French Empire.

In such circumstances England could afford to wait; for a prolonged war brought no dangerous drain of human material; the loss of money and dislocation of trade were in a long view far more than compensated by the acquisition of overseas territory, which gradually transformed the island kingdom into the world-circling empire. Such wars were indeed bound to be long wars, as in each case the dominating power, against which the coalition strove, was both better prepared than its adversaries, and was able to use its lesser allies practically as the instruments of its own unfettered will. In consequence history went far to prove that British success in the great continental struggles was due, not to the adoption of any continental model of strategy, but to the deliberate maintenance of her own liberty of action. The alliances which she created or entered aimed rather at securing common political results than at waging war with any concerted unity of direction. This statement is no doubt less true of the War of the Spanish Succession than of the Napoleonic War, because Marlborough in the former was able to exercise a unique personal influence over the members of the coalition, as being both their foremost soldier and diplomatist.

Still, generally speaking, it is true that British influence over continental wars has not been to determine their strategy in the narrower sense, but rather their general course and character. And this is so just because in naval as opposed to military strategy we have maintained our choice and control practically unfettered.

Moreover, it will be the main thesis of these chapters to prove that in the years 1914–18 the same generalisation in its broad lines holds good. Although, contrary to all earlier precedent, our contribution in men and our losses were on a scale comparable with, if not absolutely equal to, those of our principal allies and antagonists, yet our actual share in the determination of Allied strategy on land remained surprisingly small. On the other hand, it is profoundly true that our policy at sea alone enabled a great deal of that continental strategy to be put into force at all.

II

At this point it is well to stop and ask whether it is not begging the question to speak of Allied strategy at all in the late war. Would it not be more accurate to speak of a partial and incomplete co-ordination of separate efforts? This is of course perfectly true. It is a defect to a certain degree inevitable in every coalition, but particularly in the Entente where at least three powers, the British Empire, France and Russia, could justly claim a position of complete equality. The strategy of a coalition will always consist to a large extent in badly synchronised compromises, and can never hope to rival in efficiency a single direction, or even a single preponderating will. "After all Napoleon was not such a great general, he only had to fight against coalitions." Such was the outburst of General Sarrail at Salonika when, in command of the armies of five nations, he was contending in miniature against all the political and military divergencies of the countries represented.

But if all this is admitted, it would be unfair to deny that a closer co-operation was actually achieved between the members of the Entente than between the members of any earlier comparable coalition. This may be explained by three reasons:

(i) All its members did sincerely desire the same thing, "the destruction of the military domination of Germany", to use the familiar words so often in the mouths of war-time statesmen.

(ii) The geographical position of the Entente, which as the Germans so bitterly insisted had been exploited for their *Einkreisung* in the previous decade, dictated naturally a convergent form of siege pressure. Such a concentric attack on Russia or on France under the conditions of the modern world is almost impossible. On the

[5]

other hand the geographical setting of Russia condemned her to practical isolation.

(iii) The Great War was the first of its kind in which all information on all fronts was—at least in its broad outlines—available for everyone practically simultaneously. It was therefore possible to arrange for the synchronisation and succession of blows in accordance with mutual need. Every move on the chess-board could be made in reliance on up-to-date information. A century ago, however anxious a statesman or general might be to help, he was bound to hesitate before acting on stale news, one, two or three months out-of-date. A study of Wellington's campaign in France, 1813–14, shows how enormously he was hampered by the slow percolation of news from the German theatre. The Russians in particular between 1914 and 1916 showed an extraordinary readiness to stage "relief offensives" at a moment's notice. The very fact of their improvisation, however, made them almost always sadly ineffective and costly. Moreover, except for the Russians, all the great chiefs of the Entente, civil and military, could meet at almost a day's notice to discuss their mutual problems, and to pool their experiences.

Allied strategy then must be understood as a loose and approximate but far from meaningless term. Even among the Central Powers there were many divergencies from the strict ideal of centralised effort; indeed the rift between Falkenhayn and Conrad in the winter of 1915–16 cut deeper than that between any two chiefs of the Entente, and barely missed the most disastrous consequences.

So the British influence will be considered in proportion to its share in shaping or co-ordinating the Allied effort, and in relation to the strategy of one or more members of the Entente. It is indeed obvious that at any given moment these two points may be entirely distinct. For example, in 1916 a plan was made for co-ordinating all the offensives of the Entente, French, British, Russian and Italian. There was also at the same time the wholly Franco-British problem of the correct strategy to be employed in the projected attack in France.

III

It is hard to define the role of strategy in modern war, to decide the limits wherein it begins and ends. War is no longer in essence an act of policy, "a continuation of policy by other means", but a supreme effort to break the resistance of the whole enemy population. As Hindenburg truly said, "the side with the best nerves will win". Every kind of measure, whatever its political, financial or economic consequences, may be justified on military grounds alone as essential for winning the war. Briand might well complain that "modern war is too serious a business to be entrusted to soldiers". But the monstrous paradox remains true that the more important the war, the less say the responsible statesmen among the belligerents are likely to have in waging it. In Germany the victory of strategy as determined by soldiers over policy was almost absolute. The invasion of Belgium demanded by the Schlieffen plan made certain the very result that the statesmen most dreaded, the immediate entry of England. The plan of mobilisation had been so drawn up without any alternative scheme that, however anxious France might have been to evade her treaty commitments with Russia, Germany would have been forced instantly to declare war upon her. As everyone knows the unrestricted submarine campaign was forced through by the general staff in spite of Bethmann-

Hollweg's resistance, who foresaw the consequences of provoking the United States beyond remedy. Conversely, an official pronouncement of the unqualified readiness of Germany to give up Belgium was vetoed by the military and naval experts, who declared that it was necessary to retain large portions of it. Yet such a statement would have gone farther to weaken England's war will and to forward the opening of negotiations than anything else. Nor was this unrecognised by the successive Chancellors, who nevertheless sealed their lips. It needed indeed but a word from the High Command to overthrow them.

It is clear that the Germans, sentimental, submissive, hierarchical and desperate, welcomed the almost absolute and all-embracing domination of strategy.

It would, however, be quite untrue to suggest that either in England or France such or even analogous conditions prevailed.

On the contrary the statesmen of both countries were as a rule resolute in refusing a military demand, the consequences of which they considered politically disastrous or immoral. For example, the vehement demands that cotton should be placed at once on the list of absolute contraband was delayed until it was certain that such an action would not cause a breach with the United States. Dutch neutrality was not violated in order to use the Scheldt for the help of the beleaguered garrison at Antwerp. It is perhaps only in the treatment of Greece and Persia that the civil authorities bowed to military pressure against their own better judgment. The terms of alliance offered as an inducement to Italy and Rumania, which were in many respects contradictory to the principles for which the Allies declared themselves to be fighting, were of course prompted by assumed military necessity, but those who negotiated them took full responsibility for their actions. They cannot be considered as in any way due to the dictation of professional soldiers. Both had in fact consequences which at least some professional soldiers foresaw and deplored.

If, then, we may allow that the British Cabinet, with which we are primarily concerned, maintained its ascendancy in the sphere which most properly belonged to it, it remains to consider to what extent it could influence the course of strategy proper.

Now it is clear that in former wars the British Cabinet had exercised an effective and sometimes arbitrary control over strategy itself. It had been the Cabinet, often without reference to military opinion, which had decided how and where the armed forces were to be employed. The general in command had been nothing more than the executant of orders given to him. Unless his prestige and influence were unusually high he had little to say even on the questions of the means placed at his disposal. Even Wellington had little control of the officers selected for high commands in his army. This was partly because no general staff existed in England until 1904; a deliberate policy of successive governments, which feared the influence of highly trained technical advisers. Moreover, the Army, as Fortescue points out not without some exaggeration, was always a secondary and neglected instrument, which received small encouragement to make itself efficient, especially in its higher branches. A greater latitude, though within narrow limits, had always been allowed to the "sure shield" of the Navy.

Tradition therefore suggested that the Cabinet would retain the initiative and exercise a rigid

control over strategy in the Great War. Moreover, their responsibility for human life was on
a far vaster scale than ever before. In all more
than six million men were mobilised from the
British Isles. Again, for the first time British
ministers were ultimately responsible for the
employment of great bodies from every part of
the Empire. Another three and a quarter million
men had been enrolled overseas. The casualties
of the Australians and Canadians amounted in
each case to almost 300,000, or considerably
more than those of the U.S.A.

Would it not therefore be supposed that these
enormous responsibilities, to which ministers
were fully alive, which indeed, as we know,
obsessed some of them with a feeling of blood-
guiltiness, would have naturally led to an even
tighter control over the strategy of the war?

But in effect the contrary result happened.
This was due to several causes. First, it invariably
happens that when the majority of able-bodied
men become temporary soldiers they tend almost
unconsciously to exalt the military and depress
the civilian prestige. This was noticed with
surprise in the days of the first national army
during the French Revolution, among men who

at the moment of enlistment had been exalted by the idea of citizenship. This feeling is not only acquiesced in but often exaggerated by the civilians themselves from a kind of apologetic shame for not being themselves in uniform. It is in modern times naturally inflamed by the Press, which loves to create splendid figures of heroic resolution and imperturbable sagacity, who are contrasted with the wobbling and irresolute politicians. Moreover, the mechanism of modern war is so intensely technical and complicated, it is so deeply embedded in the ratio of tonnage to men, the capacity of roads and railways, the proportion of shells to guns, of guns to men, etc., etc., that the amateur can be led by the staff officer into a complicated maze of bewilderment, and lost there, whenever that result is desired. Modern war tends inevitably to deaden the expert mind and to kill imagination. It might be supposed that generals when confronted with the flankless fortified line would be driven to use more rather than less imagination. This might have been so, had not the creation of this continuous fortification accumulated such a vast mass of men and materials. To have shifted any considerable proportion elsewhere would have meant enormous effort and a great risk. These might have been taken had it not been for the fact that every great Allied country was by then turning out or able to secure almost inexhaustible supplies of every engine of war. It became therefore the line of least resistance to reduce strategy to massed tactics and to essay to break through the opposing line by brute force. If one million shells are not enough try five, if not five then try ten. The French actually used eleven millions in nine days in one of their least successful efforts on the Chemin des Dames in 1917. Moreover, as soon as a speedy end of the war became obviously unrealisable, Entente strategy was naturally drawn towards the so-called "war of attrition", as it was optimistically and tendentiously called, just because the man-power and the resources belonging to or available for the Allies were so much greater than those of the Central Powers. If your adversary's assets are conceived of as constantly diminishing in proportion to your own, it is unnecessary to think out any imaginative scheme for defeating him. "Hard pounding" will do it in time—and time does not matter. It is obvious that when strategy is thus reduced to tactics the civilian must be left in gasping bewilderment, and the staff is supreme.

When therefore we seek to assess the British influence on Allied strategy, it must be mainly understood to be the influence of the ideas of British on Allied soldiers. British ministers, Churchill and Lloyd George in particular, had many schemes for fighting the war in an entirely different way from the course which it actually took. It is very far from certain that all these schemes would have been wise or practical, but it is perfectly certain that they never received an impartial examination. They were invariably buried in a mass of technical objections, or pontifically declared to be contrary to elementary maxims of military prudence. This does not imply any insincerity on the part of those who used such arguments, but merely—what everyone knows —that if your mind is already committed to one course it will always be fertile in conclusive arguments to show the impossibility of taking another.

It would be very interesting to speculate on the probable effects of some of the alternative plans for winning the war put forward by British statesmen. But it would be quite impossible to do so at any length within the scope of this book, which must be mainly confined to the far narrower question of what British influence proved in fact to be.

IV

It is necessary to ask in a few preliminary words what influence the probability of British intervention exercised upon the war plans of France and Russia. Obviously it gave those two countries greater confidence to accept the risks of a conflagration. But did it do anything more definite? With regard to Russia the answer can be given at once. The plans of the Russian staff were drawn up quite independently of any action which this country might take. The utmost that can be said is that the naval convention between the two admiralties (it had no binding political force) seems to have considered the contingency of a Russian landing in Pomerania, if the British fleet penetrated into the Baltic, and gained an ascendancy there.

As regards France the commitments of honour were, of course, far more definite and had been technically worked out. General Michel, indeed, who preceded Joffre as Vice-President of the Council of War, had been much impressed with the probability that British aid would prolong the war to the advantage of the Dual Alliance, if France could resist the first *attaque brusquée*. He had therefore drawn up a plan envisaging the defensive on the whole Western Front. Joffre, however, his successor in 1913, who preached the doctrine of the *offensive à outrance*, which had become an almost irrational profession of faith among his younger staff officers, and accepted the almost universal estimate of a short war, substituted the notorious plan No. 17. This of course provided for the alignment of six British divisions on the French left wing, the attack of which was left to the last in order to secure our co-operation. But no alternative plan had been drawn up to meet the case of Britain's refusal to participate, or to mobilise simultaneously, and the scheme of attack would have been put into operation none the less. Therefore it is plain— though the contrary has often been stated—that the French did not depend upon British support. They merely hoped for it in order to attack with brighter prospects of success, just as they hoped also for Italian neutrality. The British staff had no official knowledge of plan No. 17; and had merely arranged to put the B.E.F., if ordered abroad, in the region of Maubeuge to operate in support of the French wing. There is no evidence to suggest that it was ever known whether such support would be offensive or defensive in character.

It may, however, be noted that the probability of our support prevented the French Government from considering the plan favoured by Joffre of marching the French 4th army through the northern region of Belgian Luxembourg. This manœuvre, as he correctly pointed out, would provide a far more favourable terrain for attack than the broken, blind and wooded country of the Ardennes, the only possible area of advance if Belgian neutrality were respected, and where in fact Ruffey met with headlong overthrow.

While, then, the expectation of British aid had scarcely any influence on the French dispositions by land, it was far otherwise with the strategical disposition of the fleet. It had been arranged between the two admiralties that French naval concentration should be in the Mediterranean, and British in the North Sea. Such a concentration had obvious advantages for France. It

practically secured the command of the Mediterranean, made it still more unlikely that Italy
would depart from the implied promise of
neutrality made by Prinetti in 1902, and would
ensure the immediate passage to France of the
seasoned Algerian army corps together with
subsequent reinforcements of coloured troops.
But it left the northern coast of France either
undefended or to be defended by the British
Navy. As the arrangement was the result of a
definite understanding with the British Admiralty it really came little short of an absolute,
if informal, guarantee that the British Navy
would protect the French shores in the event of
a German attack. It was therefore a far more
important pledge of British intervention than
the military conversations, the importance of
which interested writers like Repington and
Wilson have consciously exaggerated. Grey
himself recognised this when he assured Cambon
on August 1 that the British Navy would oppose
the Germans if they came through the Channel
to attack French ports and shipping. It is true
that this assurance was given subject to the assent
of Parliament, and was also compatible, though
barely so, with British neutrality, if Germany

2-2

agreed, as she promised to do on August 3, to such a restriction upon her naval activities.

As regards Belgium, it is probable that the Barnardiston-Jungbluth conversations, and the conviction that must have resulted therefrom that England would not merely support Belgian resistance, but would use her alleged treaty rights of landing troops without invitation, should Belgium acquiesce in military aggression, must have gone far to fortify the Belgian Cabinet in support of King Albert's determination to uphold by force the guaranteed neutrality of 1839. It is definitely stated by Joffre (*Memoirs*, 1, 109), who was presumably in a position to know, that the reinforcement of the garrison of Liége by an active division was due to the intervention of Sir Henry Wilson.

v

Neither the British Cabinet nor the naval and military staffs had worked out any definite scheme for waging a continental war in concert with a European coalition against the Central Powers. What had been done, and done very thoroughly thanks to Lord Haldane, Churchill and Fisher, was to take those steps which were considered indispensable for the security of the British Islands and the Empire in the event of our being involved in a war with Germany.

On the military side the Expeditionary Force of six divisions had been admirably equipped, and provided with a fair pool for reserves through the creation of the army and special reserves. It had been morally earmarked, if this expression is permissible, for immediate co-operation with France. There was, however, no binding engagement that a single division should be sent abroad, or if so should prolong the French line. At the Council of War held on August 5 French proposed that the force should be sent to Antwerp, and the actual decision taken was to despatch immediately only four instead of the six divisions available. For Home Defence a force of fourteen divisions had been organised in the Territorials, amounting to some 270,000 men. It had probably been expected that a proportion of them would be available as drafts for the Regular Army, as recruits had been asked, though not pressed, to volunteer for foreign service. Only some 20,000 men had in fact taken this pledge.

The reorganisation of the Indian army under Haig made it possible to hope that some military contribution might be expected from there. The Government of India, however, at the time of the outbreak of war was definitely averse from any large effort and doled out military expenditure on a most penurious scale. The self-governing Dominions had been informed without reserve at the recent Imperial Conferences of the precarious position in Europe and had been stimulated to reorganise their own naval and military defences. They were, however, under no obligation to send any contingent overseas.

It is clear, then, that from a military as opposed to a naval standpoint it was completely uncertain what part the British Empire would play in a European war. One thing alone was certain. If the war proved in accordance with general anticipation to be short, our military role would necessarily be very much restricted. This is indeed foreshadowed in the Cabinet instructions given to French on his departure.

It must be recognised from the outset that the numerical strength of the British Force, and its contingent reinforcements, is strictly limited, and with this consideration kept steadily in view it will be obvious that the greatest care must be exercised towards a minimum of losses and wastage. Therefore, while every effort must be made to coincide most sympathetically with the plans and wishes of our Ally, the gravest consideration will devolve upon you as to participation in forward movements, when large bodies of French troops are not engaged and where your Force may be unduly exposed to attack.

It was, however, believed that the equilibrium between the French and German forces in the West was so close that the highly trained Expeditionary Force, reckoned to be much superior in quality to any conscript army, might turn the scale. Limited then as our contribution avowedly was, it might nevertheless prove decisive. For it was commonly held that if Germany failed to obtain an immediate decision in the West she must be speedily defeated by the threefold pressure of the French and Russian armies and of the British fleet.

The concentration of the fleet in the North Sea had been made, as we have seen, by arrangement with France, but it was prompted by self-preservation, and its dispositions were entirely unfettered. It is indeed certain that we should have relinquished supremacy in the Mediterranean, even had the French refused to place their main strength there. It has been said without exaggeration that the most decisive event of the war took place before it was declared; this was the double order to keep the Grand Fleet together at the conclusion of the test mobilisation on July 26 and to take up War Stations by steaming secretly out of the Channel on July 29. This secured both the country against invasion and the despatch of the Expeditionary Force, and made possible the gradual improvisation of that remorseless economic strategy, which finally went so far to strangle our principal adversary.

It may therefore be claimed that the British entry into the war in the actual circumstances in which it took place was of decisive moment for the Entente, as, indeed, the Kaiser prophetically and poignantly noted. For

(i) It is almost certain, though not susceptible of proof, that the B.E.F. saved France from decisive defeat in 1914.

(ii) Time was thus given for the development of the resources of the British Empire and the Allies, opportunity for the enormous financial and economic assistance of America, and for the imposition and elaboration of the blockade.

(iii) The British participation changed the character of the war from a European to a World conflict. Further, our naval supremacy alone made possible the various amphibious expeditions (over and above the immense task of maintaining and supplying the B.E.F.), which have been condemned on the one hand as noxious "side-shows" and regretted on the other for their timidity and inadequacy.

(iv) Finally, it was due to the Royal Navy and to the Mercantile Marine that the American Army was brought over in sufficient numbers by the summer of 1918 to save the Entente, if not from irretrievable defeat, at least from a precarious defensive throughout that year and from the indefinite prolongation of the war into the abyss of universal chaos.

VI

It will be convenient to consider the campaign of 1914 by itself, both because it forms a complete drama of open warfare and because British military influence was strictly confined to the

Western theatre. The importance of the B.E.F. itself was, with two exceptions, confined to the tactical role which it played in those three months of furious conflict. But it so happened that its tactical position almost throughout involved questions of the highest strategical importance. This doubtless is likely to happen to any army, where vast plans are being adapted or improvised on the great chess-board of a wide-flung moving battle. Each one of the French armies found itself in positions where a tactical failure might involve a general strategical crash. (Ludendorff indeed has said that in modern war "tactics must always govern strategy".) But it seems true that none of the armies under Joffre's direction was so constantly placed in situations which involved the very core of decision as the B.E.F. Contrary to general belief the German army was slightly outnumbered in the battle of the frontiers, for it counted 78 divisions against 85 (74 French, 5 British by August 26 and 6 Belgian). But its superiority on the right wing was enormous, for 54 German divisions wheeled north of Thionville to oppose 23 French.

It is therefore true that the presence of the

British force as a prolongation of the French left flank was of literally inestimable value. Without it Lanrezac might well have been completely rolled up, with the probable loss of the whole 5th army. As is well known, Kluck himself after the war repeatedly gave to British officers the most emphatic and generous testimony to this effect: "Without the incomparable British Army I should have taken Paris." Whether such a catastrophe would have involved the immediate disappearance of France from the war cannot be determined.

Again we have it on the authority of Bülow, commanding the 2nd German army, and of Kuhl, chief of staff to Kluck, that it was the crossing of the Marne by British columns on the morning of September 9 which forced the general retreat of all the armies as far as Verdun. It is perfectly true that French's tactics during the advance were both timid and dilatory, and that the British share in the victory was due to its position and not to its enterprise. It was indeed due to Joffre's personal and impassioned entreaty that French agreed to move at all. Nor would he have remained in any kind of contact with the French armies if Kitchener had not at his famous visit ordered him to do so. Yet its position in front of the gap between Kluck and Bülow was of such vital importance that Joffre's plan would have been not so much ruined as meaningless, if French had persevered in his original intention to withhold all co-operation.

It may also be noted that some days before the German retreat was ordered Moltke had already become nervous at the landing of a British marine brigade at Ostend on August 25. This force was estimated by the German general staff at 40,000 men, and a half-belief was accorded to the mysterious rumour, which originated in England, of an army corps of Russians transported from Archangel into Belgium. As these troops were believed to be about to co-operate with the Belgian field army still intact in its secure lair at Antwerp, alarm had already penetrated the nervous offices at Luxembourg of a dangerous thrust at the communications of the right wing. Moltke was indeed despondent and meditating retreat even before he sent Colonel Hentsch on his famous mission.

This same Belgian flank was again the scene early in October of another strategical stroke which, feeble and fumbling as it was, proved of momentous consequence. Both Joffre and French, absorbed in the so-called "race to the sea", had desired that Antwerp should be left to her impending fate, for in their eyes she would soon be recovered, when the encircling tip of the Allied line had outflanked the German right in the north. Actually the network of railways in Northern France enabled the enemy to thrust out his own threatening wing betimes. The marines and the untrained, unequipped fragments of the Royal Naval division sent by Churchill to Antwerp prolonged the resistance of the dying fortress for at least two days; while Rawlinson's corps operating round Bruges and Ghent just enabled the dispirited Belgian army to creep back to the Yser. Time is everything in war, and there is a large measure of agreement that these two or three days saved the Channel ports, for the possession of which, as it actually turned out, a most desperate and swaying battle of three weeks was fought. That the British army was able to be its protagonist is due to French. Lord Oxford used to say that the action of the British commander, taken entirely on his own initiative, to move his army from the Aisne to Flanders at the end of September, was one of the greatest of all services to the Allied cause, and by itself justified French's appointment. Moreover, he importuned Joffre till he extorted a grudging consent that it should be done immediately and wholesale, instead of piecemeal as the Frenchman proposed. As the British troops were admittedly the best trained in the West, and so excelled in musketry that a German official monograph credited them with twenty-eight machine guns per battalion instead of two, as they only escaped annihilation through the supremest devotion and endurance, it seems almost impossible that the Channel ports could have been saved had they remained on the Aisne. Indeed, even as it was, the line could hardly have stayed, had not the British warships continually galled the open flank of the enemy advancing over the sand-dunes. This was the first and only time that the fleet had the opportunity of directly influencing the course of land operations in the West.

Chapter II

LOST OPPORTUNITIES AND THE WAR OF ATTRITION

I

By the end of 1914 the British Empire could put forward strong claims for a preponderating, if not a decisive, voice in the councils of the Allies. For (i) after the Battle of the Falkland Islands the British Navy was supreme over the oceans, its rival being represented on the high seas by one hunted light cruiser, the *Dresden*. Consequently the Allies could confidently expect to have the whole world as their military market and to close it to their enemies. Further, the Navy was in a position to transport and maintain a large army at any point, where a strategical descent should be thought desirable, for the submarines had as yet made no inroads upon shipping.

(ii) Its wealth and unrivalled facilities for credit would carry the weaker members of the Alliance in financial safety over a long period and would make possible loans in the United States at reasonable terms.

(iii) British man-power was still almost intact (our total casualties had been about 90,000), and thanks to Kitchener the decision had already been taken to use it on a vast scale. Seventy divisions were formed or to be formed at home. The contributions from the Dominions and India had already surpassed the hopes or fears of friends or enemies. Moreover, though so great a force was in training, no commitment had been made to use any of it in France. The B.E.F., swollen by the regular divisions from India, by the Indian corps, and by a number of isolated territorial battalions, had reached the equivalent of some eleven divisions. Every available man had naturally been sent there, because the need had been so desperate, and without rival else-where; and until the line was stabilised every blow struck by the enemy in Flanders rang with almost the same note as that of an invader. It is true that French had been instructed that "the reasons which have induced H.M.G. to declare war" were to prevent or repel the invasion of French territory and to restore the neutrality of Belgium. But it is obvious that the instructions issued at the outset to the commander of an expeditionary force in no way committed the Cabinet to retain the whole or even the greater part of their future available army in France, particularly as the strategical possibilities had been changed and widened by the entry of Turkey on October 28. The object of the war was simply the destruction of the military power of Germany; the pressing question: How could this object be most speedily and securely accomplished?

The war at the beginning of 1915, as Churchill has well said, was still "manageable", and though the Allies realised that time was on their side, and began to turn the economic screw by the institution of the blockade in March, they had no intention or desire of letting the struggle degenerate into one of attrition. The policy of "Killing Germans" was gradually evolved as an excuse for the complete failure of that year, and was decked up in a hopeful verisimilitude by the fantastic figures of German casualties to which such writers as Belloc gave wide publicity.

The general estimate of responsible persons in the Entente was that a victorious end could be expected in the autumn.

It was pre-eminently the year in which military operations and diplomacy should go hand in hand. The itching or vacillating neutrals on the southern and eastern flanks of the Central Powers would practically complete the great circle of siege, if they could be induced to join the right side. It was therefore of even greater importance than normally in war for each of the great Alliances to seize the initiative and to gain a spectacular success as early as possible.

Now for the first time the Entente was faced with that most momentous question: Was the war to be won in the West or in the East? It is of course true that in the autumn of 1914 there were many who hoped and perhaps believed that if the German flood could be dammed in France, the Russian steam-roller would grind its inexorable way to Berlin. But the issue in 1915 was different. It was for the Western Powers to decide whether they themselves would seek the issue in France, or through the Balkans. The theoretical advantages of the latter policy were great. For

(i) It would aim at a geographical co-ordination of Russia's effort with that of the Western Powers against the two weakest members of the

Central Alliance, Austria and Turkey. If successful in knocking out the latter, it would enable a
stream of munitions to be poured into Russia
instead of the intermittent trickle at Archangel,
and Russia's exports of grain would become
available for the West.

(ii) It would not merely impress the Balkan
neutrals but would give them the desired gage
of confidence and security by forming a common
front for their own armies with those of the
Allies.

It cannot be said that the British Cabinet or
even the War Committee (which was merely a
consultative body) had any definite policy for
1915. But its two most dynamic and vehement
personalities, Churchill and Lloyd George, were
passionate Easterners, though with different
angles of approach. Lloyd George wished to
strike at Austria direct through Dalmatia or
Salonika, Churchill to combine all the Balkans
in an invasion of Hungary concerted with
Russia, after first knocking out Turkey.
Kitchener, whose utterances, as we know from
the testimony of his colleagues, were still re-
garded as inspired oracles, expressed when
writing to French (January 2, 1915) no such

[35]　　　　　3-2

positive preference, but his definite disbelief in any decisive action in France:

The feeling is gaining ground that although it is essential to defend the lines we hold, troops over and above what are necessary for that service could be better employed elsewhere. I suppose we must now recognise that the French Army cannot make a sufficient break through the German lines of defence to cause a complete change of the situation and bring about the retreat of the German forces from Northern Belgium. If that is so, then the German lines in France may be looked upon as a fortress that cannot be carried by assault and also cannot be completely invested—with the result that the lines can only be held by an investing force, while operations proceed elsewhere.

The question of *where* anything effective can be accomplished opens a large field, and requires a good deal of study....Russia is hard pressed in the Caucasus, and can only just hold her own in Poland. Fresh forces are necessary to change the deadlock; Italy and Roumania seem the most likely providers; therefore some action that would help to bring them out seems attractive, though full of difficulties.

Whether Kitchener opened his mind to the Cabinet in a similar way seems doubtful; at least I have not found it anywhere recorded. It is certain that no orders were given to the naval and military staffs to work out plans for any such amphibious expedition.

It is indeed probable that they would not have been in a position to do so, as the Admiralty staff was at that time extremely inchoate, while that of the War Office consisted of a few sub-missive nominees of Kitchener, all the ablest brains having gone to France with the B.E.F.

In any case a Cabinet of twenty was extremely ill-fitted to take rapid or clear-cut strategical decisions, and was indeed further hampered by the great capacity of its members for argument and discussion, and by the desire of its head to harmonise discordant views by conciliatory for-mulae, which were often an excuse for inaction.

This failure of the Cabinet to make up its mind before the campaigning season started was the main reason why our influence over the plans adopted for that year was, if not negligible, at least ineffective. It is now known that a large-scale Eastern project would have received in-fluential support in France, from Briand among civilians, Galliéni, Castelnau and Franchet d'Esperey among soldiers.

To affirm that a bold attempt should have been made to win the war in the East in 1915 by no means implies that it would have been correct strategy to pursue that policy in the later years. For 1915 presented opportunities which when once lost could not be regained.

(i) From May onwards the Central Powers were committed to a great campaign with the object of crippling Russia. An analysis of that campaign shows clearly that it could not have been broken off before September. Further, I think it can be stated that it must have been recognised by the Allied staffs that the campaign was in a constant state of flux after the break through at Gorlice (May 2). Until the line was stabilised it remained so bulged, so curved, so broken that to have abandoned the moving battle in order to transfer troops to the West on any considerable scale would have been impossible for the Germans without the gravest risk of compromising the results already achieved. Therefore the West could have been organised defensively for that year without serious risk. It could have been thoroughly insured in (say) the proportions of 5 to 4, while allowing for the employment of large forces elsewhere. For in fact during this year Allied superiority in France amounted to nearly 7 to 4.

(ii) Serbia being still intact, a landing at Salonika (which would almost certainly have met with Greek acquiescence and probably with Greek support) would have enabled a direct attack to be made on the Danube. It is true that it might have taken about six months to create the communications necessary for the advance of a considerable army (say 12–15 divisions together with the Serbs). If this work had been started in January the campaign could have begun in earnest in June, when Italy would also have begun to knock on the Isonzo. Austria's position throughout the spring was so critical that she could not have forestalled such an expedition by another attack on Serbia, where she had already failed three times with severe loss.

(iii) The submarine menace in 1915 was still in its infancy. British shipping was still actually superior in tonnage to the total at the outbreak of war, owing to the enemy tonnage captured in the harbours of the Entente. Consequently there would not have been any difficulty in transporting a large expeditionary force, and in maintaining supplies both for it and for the Serbian and Greek armies.

An attack on the Danube seems in retrospect

a better scheme than any attempt to strike at Constantinople. For (*a*) Bulgaria could not possibly have joined the Central Powers, even if she had refrained from siding with the Entente, provided that a large Franco-British army had been co-operating with Serbia. The flanks therefore would have been more secure than in the event of an advance northwards through Thrace from Gallipoli. (*b*) The Russians would have raised no objection to the Greek alliance, as they so selfishly did, when they feared lest the prize of Constantinople should be disputed as a result of such an alliance. On the other hand the shortage of guns and shells for the Army was a strong argument for using the Navy as a direct auxiliary for any expedition. It is also true that the forcing of the Dardanelles was a necessary preliminary for using the great waterway of the Danube as a basis of supply for an army attacking Austria through Serbia.

And so it is possible that Great Britain might have made a decisive contribution to the strategy of 1915, if the Cabinet had made up their minds in January what they meant by an attack on the Dardanelles and how it was to be brought to a conclusion; for until April the Turks were surprisingly ill-prepared to meet a serious blow. As it was, the expedition never threw off its origin as a naval diversion to help the Russians, for which the military forces were a grudged and belated afterthought. It remained to the end a complicated and exceedingly expensive diversion. Its effect on the war as a whole can be quickly summarised. The refusal to cut our losses after the failure at Suvla made it impossible to send timely or adequate reinforcements to Serbia. It has therefore a heavy indirect responsibility for the November overthrow of that country. On the other hand, it inflicted a crippling blow on the flower of Turkish man-power—the Turkish casualty lists revealed after the war that they had lost twice our number. It therefore made possible the eventual conquest of Palestine and Mesopotamia. It is, however, doubtful whether the war would have ended a day earlier had the British forces remained on an active defensive on the southern frontier of Palestine, and in Southern Mesopotamia.

Generally speaking, in 1915 Great Britain acquiesced in and subordinated herself to French strategy, and by so doing went far towards renouncing for the whole war her proper share in its direction, except in naval and economic policy.

The master idea of French soldiers, which reflected the passionate longing of public opinion, was to drive the enemy as quickly as possible out of the national territory. Starting from the true premise that the war on land could be lost only in France, the Higher Command proceeded to the conclusion, which at least in 1915 was unsound, that the war could be won only in France. As it was certainly necessary in the interest of Russia for the Western Allies to attack somewhere in strength in 1915, they had to attack in France, as they had renounced any great effort elsewhere. The British Army was reduced to the role of an autonomous auxiliary of France, attacking when and where the French Higher Command thought useful to help a larger French effort. French was forbidden to undertake his proposed joint operation with the Navy on the Belgian coast in January because Joffre said that it would be "eccentric". He attacked at Festubert to help Foch in Artois, he was given the grim region between La Bassée and Loos in September, a maze of dumps, slag heaps, pitheads and bristling villages, in order to enable Foch to capture the Vimy ridge. His protests and the still stronger ones of Haig, who had to do the work, were overruled.

The campaign of 1915 in the West had in fact been entirely settled and run by Joffre with disastrous results. The Franco-British armies had sacrificed at least 750,000 men for two or three small advances, which nowhere exceeded four miles, and created worse tactical positions than those previously occupied.

II

It is a curious paradox that so unfortunate an experience should have strengthened the belief of practically all military minds, French and British, in a continued offensive in the West. Yet so it was—1915 proved the year of most adventures for the Entente. After that date no new campaigns were undertaken, and the war on land definitely assumed the character which it retained until the close. What was that character? It was definitely laid down by the Chantilly Conference (December 1915) that there were three principal fronts, the Western, the Southern (or Italian) and the Eastern (or Russian), and that all others were subsidiary and should be organised defensively. These principal fronts were to be manned respectively by the Franco-British, the Italians and the Russians in practically water-tight compartments. But a real effort was made to co-ordinate their different offensives for the coming year. This was the great advance on 1915. There was to be unity of direction; the pressure to be applied upon the Central Powers was to be, broadly speaking, simultaneous; and, in spite of the preventive blows at Verdun and Trentino, it was so applied, though with much diminished power. As far as England was concerned she was permanently committed to keeping the larger part of her armies in France. But she never gave up the liberty of conducting the Mesopotamian, Palestine and African campaigns on the minimum scale which the Cabinet thought appropriate. The scale was indeed a large one for "secondary theatres". On January 1, 1918, out of 2,837,315 troops (including natives), 888,315 were employed elsewhere than in France, though of course the Indians had proved unsuitable for service there.

On the other hand, in compensation for that

qualified liberty we were compelled to maintain large forces in Salonika—in all 440,000 were employed there—to please the French. This expedition, the maintenance of which was made a *sine qua non*, being both the only example of a "side-show" run by the French, and almost the only important instance where the French politicians were able to impose their will on the soldiers in a matter of strategy.

What were the arguments which led British military chiefs consistently to support the French contention of permanently attacking in the West; arguments which left Lloyd George always unconvinced, but which in spite of the most strenuous endeavour he was unable to break in practice?

(i) By the end of 1915 the Central Powers, after their conquest of Serbia and alliance with Bulgaria, were in unrestricted enjoyment of their interior lines. It is indisputable that they could transfer troops more quickly to any theatre than the Entente, who were unable to transfer troops to Russia at all. They could therefore always threaten an attack with superior numbers in the West if the Allies endeavoured to reinforce any other theatre on the scale requisite for a break through. In practice, however, such a facility could apply only to the German Army, as Turks and Bulgars would never serve in France, and Austrians only with the greatest reluctance and in small numbers after the overthrow of Russia. This argument was an incontrovertible one for keeping in France a force sufficient to withstand any possible attack, but did it necessarily imply a great Allied offensive in France?

(ii) It is difficult to deny this after the campaign of 1915 had ended. Kitchener had always stated that his aim was to bring British military power to its maximum in the midsummer of the third year of the war, when he believed that its weight would prove decisive, even if not immediately. This aim, to his undying glory, he brought to accomplishment. It was inevitable, given the immense prestige of Joffre as Generalissimo, who was now in command of all the French armies and took care if necessary by threat of resignation that no troops should be diverted from France except the necessary dribble of decayed ill-equipped divisions to Salonika. It was inevitable also since Haig, the new commander-in-chief (December 1915), Robertson, the new C.I.G.S. and Wilson, chief

[46]

liaison officer at French Headquarters, all agreed vehemently on that policy.

(iii) It was also a matter of faith, or perhaps rather of rational belief, among both staffs that the enemy's line in France could be broken through, and his armies thereafter engaged in open warfare to their complete discomfiture. The whole problem was taken from the sphere of strategy into that of material calculation. If sufficient weight of metal could be thrown against a portion of the fortress wall, it must collapse. The role of the infantry was to occupy ground already destroyed.

The analogy with a fortress is, however, misleading for

(*a*) There is hardly any fortress in the world where the defences are so deep that the whole of one section cannot all be simultaneously destroyed. The trench line, however, in 1916 had become so complicated a system that no artillery could deal effectively at the same time with the whole of it. Haig's error in believing this to be possible was one of the principal causes for the British failure on July 1.

(*b*) In a fortress the garrison is limited and cannot be reinforced. But this condition was only possible in the West if the enemy's reserves were already exhausted, or if attacks took place simultaneously at so many points that it was impossible to reinforce all those threatened. Neither of these desiderata was even approximately obtained until the autumn of 1918.

(c) When a fortress wall is breached the whole object of the operation has been obtained. The fall of the fortress follows, and there is no immediate need for further advance or effort. But the rupture of a fortified line is only the beginning of the most arduous, difficult and delicate manœuvre, the rapid passing of large bodies of fresh men through the gap over several miles of devastated ground to exploit the victory. The weight of metal which accomplished the initial destruction itself proves the greatest enemy of the exploitation. The immobility which is necessary for a great trench attack itself makes almost impossible that rapid change to open warfare, which alone makes the former fruitful.

It is easy now to see that the great fault of the directing brains in the West was a kind of mechanical megalomania, pinning their faith to masses of men, masses of guns, masses of shells, masses of transport. "Vis consili expers mole ruit sua."

The immense ingenuity which was spent in assembling and providing for these human masses, in drawing up artillery time-tables, in aerial photography and reconnaissance would have been better employed in adapting to modern conditions three of the fundamental and closely connected principles of all successful war—surprise, economy of force, and elasticity of plan.

It may be objected that these reflections have little to do with the influence of our strategy on the war as a whole. But this is not so. If during 1915 the enthusiasm of Churchill for the discovery and utilisation of new weapons such as gas, tanks and smoke had been encouraged by the Higher Command it would have been possible next year to surprise the enemy without giving him long and ostentatious notice of our intentions. To carry out such a surprise, as Cambrai conclusively showed, far fewer men were required than for a massed set-piece like the Somme, and a much smaller ratio of casualties could be expected. Moreover, such surprise attacks would not require the vast preparations which made it so difficult to break off even an acknowledged failure; attack could be rapidly swivelled from point to point as in the autumn of 1918.

If then such new tactics had been worked out the British armies would not again have been cast for the gloomy role of settling down for months to attack an unsuitable area indicated by the French for their own convenience. Such docility was the more inappropriate as, owing to the wastage at Verdun, we undertook, contrary to the original arrangement, by far the heavier share of the burden and incurred casualties more than double those of our allies.

More important still, the economy of forces engaged in the West would have made possible the creation of a real strategic reserve. As Smuts truly pointed out next year, the small striking force which the Germans retained for that purpose had done wonders. Seven or eight divisions had been the spearhead of the destruction of Serbia in 1915, the overthrow of Rumania in 1916, and finally of the Caporetto rout next year. The Allies never had any such reserve of their own. The most they could do was to scrape some troops painfully together and send them to the point where the mischief had already been done beyond remedy. Lloyd George might well exclaim that "Too late" had always been the motto of the Entente. They had acted exactly as Demosthenes told the Athenians they habitually did in opposing the nimble Philip, like a clumsy boxer who puts up his hand to guard the place where he has just received a blow.

Who can say what would have been the effect of six or eight fresh British divisions appearing on the Isonzo at the moment of the Italian capture of Gorizia? The Austrians were just as unwilling to fight the British as the Italians the Germans, and we know what a similar force of the latter accomplished next year.

What effect on the course of the war can be ascribed to the Somme as actually fought by the British? It was of course infinitely the greatest contribution yet made by us to the war on land. Though our losses on the Somme were considerably greater than those of the enemy—about 4 to 3—it seems certain that the spirit and efficiency of the German troops were more seriously impaired than those of the British armies. This conclusion is suggested not only by the testimony of Hindenburg and Ludendorff, but by every kind of German war literature. The battle therefore contributed not to the attrition of men but to the spiritual exhaustion of the enemy.

The immediate strategic consequences were on the contrary unfortunate. The salient defending Bapaume had been so dinted and devastated that Ludendorff withdrew by March 1917 to the tremendous Siegfried line twenty miles to the East, so providently constructed during the winter. This was shorter—it provided for an economy of some eight divisions—and its straight course from Arras to Soissons robbed the Allies of their chance of hammering successfully at either side of the weakened and exaggerated salient.

It has been argued, not without plausibility, that if Joffre had not been dismissed immediately after concerting the Chantilly plan with Haig in December 1916 the German armies might have suffered decisive defeat in the spring of 1917.

This scheme certainly envisaged an attack on either side of the Somme at the beginning of February. If it had come off then it would have caught the enemy in the act of retiring from a position recognised as untenable without any completed rearward refuge; and before the Russian Revolution had in any way cleared up the Eastern situation. But it is most improbable that the attack could have started at the scheduled time for

(i) It would have allowed only eleven weeks for the armies to have been reconditioned and to absorb the large new drafts required. The British had lost 490,000 men on the Somme, and the French 550,000 at the Somme and Verdun.

(ii) Unless Haig's complaints about the inefficiency of the French northern railways were a mere dishonest pretext in order to ruin Nivelle's plans, his own testimony is a proof that no serious British attack could have been launched until the beginning of April.

(iii) The weather during February was peculiarly unfavourable to great operations. Snow, the most intense frost of the century, followed by thaw and many days of dense mist would have made a sustained effort almost impossible.

Chapter III

BEARING THE BURDEN AND
HEAT OF THE DAY

I

DECEMBER 1916 is one of the great landmarks of the war both militarily and politically. If, after the Marne, any subsequent date can be selected as the turning point it is this month.

It marked the German and American peace notes. The former, in spite of its stout assertion of invincibility, which was fully justified by the "war-map", indicated the profound uneasiness of the Central Powers at the prospect of economic exhaustion. This was further reflected by the decision of the General Staff to press instantly for ruthless submarine warfare, if these overtures were rejected. In Russia the murder of Rasputin was the first definite precursor of an imminent revolution. It marked finally the fall of Joffre, who had so long exercised an unrivalled domination over Allied strategy; and what is most important for our present purpose it marked the substitution of Lloyd George for Asquith as Premier.

Everyone will admit that the new Premier had a definite policy as to the role of statesmen in the conflict, and showed a devouring energy in attempting to carry it out.

His *idées maîtresses* appear to have been the following:

(i) In order to carry on modern war effectively "you cannot wage it with a sanhedrim". It is essential to have a small body of men freed from departmental duties, and from regular attendance in Parliament, representing all shades of national opinion, who can take and carry decisions rapidly into effect.

The British War Cabinet, of which the Committee of Public Safety was the prototype, was certainly the most effectively constructed body for the prosecution of a national war to be found in Europe. It is however true, as we shall see, that it was much more effective in organising the resources of the country than in directing or controlling the course of the war.

(ii) It was necessary for the statesmen to reassert their old supremacy over their professional servants both in determining the objects of strategy and in seeing that their orders were effectively carried out. This was indeed fully recognised in principle also by Briand. "What ought to be the attitude of the Governments towards the General Staffs; whatever might be their confidence in the General Staff—a confidence indeed fully justified—ought the Governments to abandon absolutely to them the control of operations?

"The French Government did not think so. It held, on the contrary, that it was the Government which, since they bore the whole responsibility for the conduct of the war, should take the initiative in regard to operations, it being always understood that the execution of the plan adopted should be left to the military authorities, who had the means to carry it out" (November 15, 1916).

Lloyd George constantly pointed out that this proviso left a wide door for evasion. "*We must not rest content with taking these decisions. We have still to see that they are carried out*" (November 15, 1916). Or again at the Rome Conference (December 1916), "I strongly urged that my proposal (i.e. for a joint offensive in Italy) should be examined by the General Staffs. *I pointed out, however, that this was not enough, and that it would never be carried out unless Ministers themselves took the matter in hand and insisted on its being considered favourably.*"

In spite, however, of such categorical assertions very little was actually done to reassert civil supremacy. For, as we shall see, the General Staffs, who had the profoundest mistrust for Lloyd George's ideas, took care to agree between themselves as to their own policy before any meeting of Allied statesmen took place. In this instance they had worked out the campaign for 1917 a few days before the Rome Conference.

But in one respect Lloyd George's initiative and insistence at this meeting proved of inestimable value to the Allied cause. Foreseeing the event of an Austro-German attack on Italy in 1917 he obtained an authorisation to the General Staffs "to work out (a plan) in all its technical details, including the elaboration of railway time-tables, and the arrangement for the necessary...communications". He is fully entitled to the boast that these preparations saved the Italian army after Caporetto. For while it is true that the Franco-British contingents did not defend the line of the Piave, it was their prompt arrival which put heart into the Italians to defend it themselves.

(iii) It was not enough for the Allies to synchronise their offensives on their respective fronts so as to make it difficult and dangerous for the enemy to transfer troops. A far closer co-ordination was required. There was of course no question of appointing a Generalissimo—even for the Western front—public opinion in no country would have tolerated such a step, except in the extremity of naked danger.

But Lloyd George insisted that two measures were possible and indeed long overdue.

(*a*) That the Allies should pool information and explain exactly to each other their respective military and political situation. This applied in particular to Russia, of which the other allies had but the scantiest and most inaccurate knowledge. Gilinski, for instance, the Russian military representative at G.Q.G., told Joffre in the autumn of 1915 that "he did not know the plans of the Grand Duke", or what orders had been given for war material, and could not even define exactly the conditions under which the Russian Army was fighting at the moment.

It had been to remedy this lack of liaison that Kitchener had sailed on the *Hampshire* (June 1916). One of Lloyd George's first acts as Premier was to arrange the Milner mission, and to ensure that it comprised a first-class delegation both political and military. Even so the moribund bureaucracy contrived to thwart it by a network of deceit and evasiveness.

(*b*) As a sequel he suggested that without definitely pooling resources the Allies should see that each one of them was provided with a standard of minimum equipment. This of course meant in practice that the two Western Powers, with their vast industrial resources, should divert from France such quantities of material as might be deemed necessary to bring the standards of Italy and Russia up to the level required for continuing large-scale offensives with any reasonable hope of success. Russia had in fact already received more than corruptive inefficiency and the inadequacy of her railway system could absorb. It was calculated that at the beginning of 1917 nearly 500,000 tons were congested at the port of Vladivostok, while similar vast dumps were springing up at Kola, the terminus of the Murmansk railway, recently completed at the cost of the lives of 50,000 prisoners of war. Much, however, could be done in supplying the Italians with heavy guns and shells, for at present they had received next to nothing.

The most important success in this direction actually obtained was the Allied Naval and Shipping Conference "to consider the best methods of co-ordinating Allied resources at sea". Lloyd George goes on to remark: "It is incredible that no such conference had ever been held before. In fact the Allied War directors never seemed to have realised that the transport question was at the root of most of their difficulties."

II

For a variety of reasons, amongst which the advent of Lloyd George to the supreme position was by no means the most important, the year 1917 marks a great increase of British influence over the course of the war.

(*a*) The coalition partially disintegrated during the year. After July it became increasingly clear that it would be necessary to write off Russia and Rumania. After Caporetto Italy became a liability instead of an asset. French man-power was declining towards exhaustion (at least 2,000,000 or 5 per cent. of the total population were dead, permanently disabled or prisoners). Consequently the old doctrine of attrition, with its comforting calculation of the respective number of reserves available for either side became obsolete. The weight of carrying on the war necessarily devolved more and more upon British shoulders; for our losses were still relatively small compared with the French, while our resources remained intact, without mutilation by invasion.

(*b*) The submarine campaign aimed at the heart of Britain could be repelled only by her efforts—those of the rest of the Entente combined as nothing. Therefore it depended upon the success of her defence whether the war could have been carried on at all. Moreover, even if she just warded off the danger of starvation, the balance of victory must incline strongly towards the Central Powers. For without British shipping the American Army could arrive only by belated driblets; and it might well happen that before they constituted a formidable force, the Franco-British armies might be overthrown beyond remedy in the West.

(*c*) The actual course of the campaign in France, which took a turn fatal to the career of its chief architect Nivelle, made a considerable measure of British independence not merely possible but necessary. Moreover, the growing military weakness of Turkey encouraged offensives against her in the two Asiatic theatres of war, the bearing of which on the subsequent course of the war has been hotly disputed, but was not in my opinion of serious importance. The campaign of 1917 had been worked out at Chantilly with high hopes. It had been calculated that the Central Powers would be too exhausted to forestall it by preventive blows like Verdun and Trentino. This calculation has been confirmed by the subsequent statements of Ludendorff and Hindenburg. Moreover, as the result of Brussilov's offensive in Galicia the enemy forces, not of course all German, in the East had been increased by no less than 535 battalions—perhaps 350,000 men. Consequently if an effective synchronisation of offensives could be arranged the prospects of a break through in the West and in the South seemed unusually bright. It was accordingly agreed that each of the Allies would start his attack within three

[62]

weeks of the other, beginning with the West at the beginning of February.

In the opinion of the enemy this scheme, if put into operation, would have brought about the military defeat of the Central Powers. "In spite of the seriousness of our position on the Western Front the absence of any Russian attacks in the spring of 1917 prevented a general crisis in our situation such as we had experienced in September 1916....If the Russian successes of July had occurred in April and May I do not see, as I look back, that G.H.Q. could have mastered the situation" (Ludendorff).

Actually the Allied plan was completely hamstrung for

(i) The Russian army fell into the immobility of approaching dissolution in March, as soon as the Revolution was successful.

(ii) The Italians made no move until the middle of May, a month after the French failure at Soissons. This inaction was partly due to nervousness of another Trentino assault, partly to Cadorna's sulkiness at the refusal of the Entente to respond to Lloyd George's proposal for a considerable Franco-British force to be despatched to Italy.

(iii) The substitution of Nivelle for Joffre, and the ensuing change of plans, made it impossible to fix upon an earlier date than April for the combined attack. By then its strategical significance and its tactical chances had been gravely compromised by the retreat to the Hindenburg line. So in effect the campaign of 1917 consisted of a series of isolated blows, lacking even the limited cohesion of its predecessor.

III

During the course of the year the B.E.F. was both more strictly subordinate and more independent of the French command than previously.

The experiment of placing Haig under the orders of Nivelle for the spring campaign proved unhappy. It caused serious friction between the two commanders and possibly delay in the execution of the plan. It is difficult to understand the British Premier's reasons for fathering it; especially as he denies the belief generally held that he was captivated by Nivelle's personality, and shared his dogmatic confidence in "la percée en vingt-quatre heures". The

[64]

method by which this subordination was effected is still more incomprehensible. He arranged with Briand to put Haig, a field-marshal, under a general junior in rank, who had been a colonel at the beginning of the war, and whose exploits, if brilliant, had been of purely local importance, without consulting or even informing either Haig or Robertson beforehand. It looks as if he was anxious to have his revenge for the blunt monotony with which the pair had turned down all his strategical projects. It was also a mistake to set up as a Generalissimo one who was himself personally responsible for the execution of his own operations. This mistake was not repeated a year later when Foch became the strategical director of Haig and Pétain.

In short, this six-weekly subordination did not make for efficiency, caused ill-will between the two General Staffs, and increased the difficulty of creating a real unity of command at the day of peril.

After the failure of the great French effort on the Chemin des Dames in April, followed by the dismissal of Nivelle and the widespread mutinies in their army, the military policy to be adopted by the British for the remainder of the campaigning season became of prime importance. Though neither the Russians nor still less the French could be written off as incapable of any further offensive action, it was clear that nothing effective could be expected of either for months. No success which the Italians unaided were likely to win would draw any appreciable portion of German power to the Isonzo.

The B.E.F., on the other hand, reached its highest strength in June 1917. The man-power situation, if not satisfactory, would allow for large operations on the scale of the previous year, if the net of conscription could be tightened. Consequently the circumstances made it imperative for Great Britain to lead and determine the immediate course of the war.

The following courses were possible:

(*a*) To adopt the avowed intention of Pétain "to wait for America and the tanks"; by which he meant to adopt a generally defensive attitude for at least a year, varied by carefully planned local operations like Messines (June), Verdun (August), Malmaison (October). To such a policy there were very grave objections. It would risk handing back to the enemy the initiative in the West, which it was hoped had been finally wrested from him after the failure at Verdun. To be able to determine when, where and for how long you will strike is a great advantage; a defensive implies a humbling submission to the enemy's will. (On the other hand it must be remembered that the initiative in the West had so far meant the subjection of the commander to the tyranny of his own enormous inelastic plans.)

Again, would it be safe to assume that the French army could repel the attacks which the enemy might launch against it, if the B.E.F. did not draw large forces to itself by the magnet of attack? We do not indeed know how frankly Pétain revealed the details of the mutinies to G.H.Q.; probably a good deal was concealed. It has, however, been stated by those in touch with Haig during the autumn that Pétain sent him frequent appeals until October to continue the battle.

Finally, the submarine menace continued very urgent throughout the summer. Doubtless it had reached its peak in April. The gradual adoption of the convoy system was producing good, though not spectacular, results. Lloyd George had shown great courage in insisting upon its trial; it is, I believe, the only instance in the war in any country where a civilian over-ruled his responsible professional advisers on a technical point. Yet who could affirm that Great Britain could afford to gamble on a year's respite from starvation, if the army waited passively for the Americans, who might be unable to cross in strength for lack of shipping?

(*b*) To attack on a scale meant to be decisive but with the new tactical methods of surprise which the able young heads of the tank corps, Elles and Fuller, were working out so fruitfully. As Cambrai proved, this was infinitely the best chance of breaking through the whole hostile system at a stroke with the greatest economy of human life. (The casualties for the first day of Cambrai have been reckoned at about 4000.) The opportunities for exploiting such a success were great. Divisions could be kept closely in hand, and could move rapidly forwards over a terrain unscarred by the explosions of millions of shells. Even the cavalry might win their legendary opportunity in open country.

Such a scheme was contemptuously rejected as a first choice; it was picked up as a forlorn hope at the very end of the season, carried through by tired troops with scanty reserves, at the moment which ensured the enemy several undisturbed months to reflect on and profit by its lessons.

Such procedure sounds like incomprehensible idiocy. Why then was it followed? Why did G.H.Q. so obstinately insist upon (*c*) the grandiose attack in Flanders, the culmination of offensive deliberation and mechanical fury?

The main answer, no doubt, is the tyranny exercised by a preconceived plan upon rigid and unimaginative minds. The Northern offensive had figured in 1916 as an alternative to complete failure on the Somme. The mines of Messines were ready to go off at least a year before their actual explosion. It had been included from the outset in the agreed programme for 1917. Haig and Robertson, who had but the faintest faith in Nivelle's glowing prophecies, had early marked it out as the *pièce de résistance* for that year. It had become an article of belief long before it was launched.

Moreover, the tank corps was a new creation, without influence and without senior officers. It was impossible for its protagonists to enforce their conviction that the proper handling of their machines would amount to a tactical revolution in trench warfare. In fact the greater their insistence the greater the natural jealousy of the older arms of the service. The tank was to be employed as an adjunct to the infantry in the way which would fit in best with the old methods of mounting an attack. It must not be allowed to dictate, manœuvre or to determine the choice of ground. A similar jealousy of the Air Force retarded its emancipation from the restrictive shackles of the Army and Navy respectively, both desirous of using it as their servant.

Finally, there was the argument so crudely expressed in its popular form, "The Army must win the war before the Navy loses it."

It does not appear that the Cabinet at any stage adopted the view that the capture of Ostend and Zeebrugge by the B.E.F. was essential to prevent a peace of humiliation in the autumn. It is certain that Lloyd George never even inclined to that opinion. He consistently maintained that the Navy could and must find its own preventive measures against the submarine. But the pressure which came from the Admiralty was undoubtedly very great. There is much evidence that Jellicoe had lost his nerve and fallen into the grip of unrelieved pessimism. It is very strange that he should have encouraged the army in this desperate venture without preparing any naval blow against their destructive nests. His only contribution was the abortive scheme for landing 20,000 men on the coast itself contingent on an advance of twelve miles from the Ypres lines.

Even on June 19 Jellicoe "stated categorically that unless that (i.e. the clearing of the Flemish coast) was done, the position would become impossible and that unless we cleared the Germans out of Zeebrugge this year, we could not go on with the war next year through lack of shipping. This startling and reckless declaration", says Lloyd George, "I challenged indignantly but the First Sea Lord adhered to it" (L.G. 2161–2).

The decision to play every available card at Ypres made impossible the fourth alternative of limited but vigorous holding attacks in France, and despatching a moderate force of (say) eight divisions to Italy. This almost certainly would have led at least to the resounding, if strategically barren, capture of Trieste—even as it was the Austrians were at their last gasp in August—and would have made the rout of Caporetto quite impossible. In retrospect such a course, which is roughly that urged by Lloyd George in June and July, appears the wisest.

No satisfactory explanation has ever yet been given for the persistence in the Ypres attack after its strategical failure was clear to demonstration and the battlefield had been reduced to an irremediable quagmire. It has been stated on good authority that Haig was obsessed with the determination to exhaust the enemy before the arrival of the Americans in such strength that their intervention might reduce Great Britain to a secondary role. He was certainly fed with a stream of misleading intelligence reports, which insisted upon the vastness of the enemy's losses and his growing deterioration. Actually the British lost in men about 5 to 3 and in officers at least 7 to 3. Nor was Ludendorff prevented from using his strategic reserve first to capture Riga, which ensured the Bolshevik Revolution and a speedy peace in the East, secondly to rout the Italians and force important diversions of Franco-British troops to Italy at the moment when the Entente was being definitely reduced to the defensive in the West.

Moreover, although Lloyd George did not then know that Haig had concealed from him the disapproval expressed both by Pétain and Foch for the Flemish enterprise, his distrust of the British generalship was keenly whetted, and had, as we shall see, important consequences during the next few months.

Chapter IV

THE LAST PHASE

I

FROM now until its close the war is governed by the realisation of Germany that her allies were on the brink of exhaustion, and that she herself must inevitably fall into the abyss, if a decisive victory could not be forced by the autumn of 1918. It was no longer possible for the diminishing success of the submarines to impose any time limit on the economic resistance of Great Britain. The entry of the United States had closed almost every loophole for the blockade, the activities of its Navy made the work of patrolling wider and more efficient. The grip which the British Navy had so tenaciously maintained on the throat of its enemies had now become a strangle-hold.

But to conjure this spectre of impending ruin Germany had for the first time since war began an almost free hand.

Russia and Rumania were knocked out, and required no more than an army of economic exploitation, few units of which needed to possess any fighting value. Italy was crippled for an indefinite period. Miserable as was the plight of the Turk after the capture of Jerusalem, it could be expected that the Entente would spare no strength for a further blow while the issue remained in the balance in the West. War weariness in itself would not suffice to detach either Turk or Bulgar from their infeudation as long as Germany retained a serious hope of victory.

In the last resort it was the British fleet which drove Ludendorff to assemble his masses of offence in Artois and Picardy.

II

How far did the Entente recognise this peril, and what was the British share in preparing against it?

The minds of the British military chiefs passed with the greatest reluctance to the idea of defence. On October 8 Haig confidently prophesied a decisive attack for 1918, even on the assumption of Russia's total defection and of the continued inability of the French to undertake great operations. On November 19 Robertson, faced with the Bolshevik Revolution and the Italian collapse, considered the utmost restriction of our operations for the following year would be:

(*a*) Keeping the initiative in our hands, so as to prevent the enemy from attacking us at any time and place of his own choosing.

(*b*) Assisting our Allies, directly or indirectly, if they are attacked.

(*c*) Continuing the pressure on the Western Front, which has hitherto had such good effect upon the interior condition of Germany.

It was not until December 3 that G.H.Q. definitely recognised that the shortage of manpower, and the probability that the enemy would transfer larger forces from the East than had been anticipated, made a defensive policy clearly necessary.

It is most improbable in any event that Lloyd George, after the bitter experience of the autumn, would have sanctioned another attack with the dice thus weighed against the Entente. The combined effect of Passchendaele and Caporetto upon the British Premier was to provoke him to further strenuous efforts to secure the following objects:

(i) To create a concrete inter-allied body with a definite and direct responsibility for carrying on the war in common on the analogy of the British War Cabinet.

(ii) To ensure that such a body would have the real strategical direction, by having at its disposal the services of technical advisers, who could act independently of the respective chiefs of staff and commanders-in-chief.

(iii) As a corollary, to create a central interallied reserve, which would be in a position to intervene anywhere immediately, and which, being at the disposal of the Supreme War Council, could not be squandered in advance at the will of any individual commander.

(iv) To attack the enemy in his weakest spot, the so-called policy of "knocking the props from under Germany".

(v) To bridle Haig, whom he profoundly distrusted but did not venture to dismiss, by allowing him no more troops than he thought necessary for defence. And further, a decision which came to maturity by degrees, to break up the partnership between Robertson and the Commander-in-Chief by substituting for the former a soldier more congenial to himself in temperament and outlook.

It remains to consider what practical effect upon the conduct of the war followed.

The Supreme War Council, in so far as it consisted of a Prime Minister and a colleague from each of the great allies, could obviously not hope to meet frequently or even to hold regular sessions. In effect no real change was made. But as Lloyd George and Clemenceau (who came into power in November) both remained at the head of their respective states till the end of the war, as both had an unshakable will to win, their growing intimacy and mutual understanding led to a more fundamental cooperation between the two Governments on a basis of real equality than had previously existed. Italy after Caporetto had to play the humble role of the poor relation; America was politically unrepresented, except during the short intervals of Colonel House's visits to Europe.

The influence of the new board of military advisers upon the campaign proved negligible. Dominated by Foch, the French chief of staff, it never fulfilled the intention of its creator, as an independent strategic inter-allied council. Deprived of the proposed strategic reserve, the formation of which was prevented by Haig's refusal to contribute his quota, its function in the critical days before the March disaster was little more than that of a military debating society. Events moved too swiftly for it. When the bitterly vexed question as to how much of the French line was to be taken over by the B.E.F. was referred to it, Haig and Pétain made a private arrangement before a decision had been given. Similarly, the two commanders agreed among themselves as to mutual support if attacked, rather than depend upon a reserve not controlled by themselves, the position of which would be determined by the war games which Sir Henry Wilson, the British representative, was playing with such gusto at Versailles. Though the arrangements made were of a very incomplete and grudging character, it is not surprising that the two commanders preferred their own understanding to the uncovenanted mercies of an uncontrolled Committee.

The real importance of the Committee was that it prepared the public mind in this country for the creation of a Generalissimo in March. It was a useful, perhaps a necessary, stage towards the attainment of that beneficent end. After its establishment the Committee, with much less ambitious aims, did much useful and unostentatious work in co-ordinating the economic and shipping policy of the Allies, but exercised no influence upon the course of the campaign.

So far it is manifest that Lloyd George's projects, if comparatively fruitless, produced some result of modest value. But his advocacy of an offensive in Palestine, and his retention of considerable forces in England, were extremely dangerous. His argument was plausible. The Allies had vainly endeavoured to break through in the West for the last three years; their superiority had been often more than 3 to 2, never less than 5 to 4. Therefore he was convinced that if, as was calculated, and as actually happened in March, men and guns on either side were approximately equal, defensive security was amply safeguarded. This doubtless would have been true if the enemy had followed the old consecrated method of deliberate ostentatious preparation. But if he attained surprise, and followed up that surprise by new tactical methods, the whole assumption was falsified. Even if it was not certain that the enemy would attack with all his might, it was at least extremely probable. If so, it was a wild gamble to divert or withhold troops. The maxim that you cannot be too strong at the decisive point is absolutely sound, provided you can be reasonably certain where and when the decision will be attempted. Whatever might be the effect of a decisive victory over Turkey upon a dispirited Germany, impotent to strike herself, it was clear to demonstration that if the Germans were in Amiens, they would scornfully neglect the entry of Allenby into Damascus. Moreover, the only great Allied pool of reserves now lay in America. It was madness to risk the disintegration, if not the complete overthrow, of the Franco-British armies before the United States had cast more than a minimal fraction of their enormous strength into the scale.

It is, of course, true that no troops were in fact despatched to Allenby, but none were withdrawn from him. He remained therefore on the compromised footing of a limited offensive capacity, unable on his own showing to do much more than consolidate his position round Jerusalem, but stronger than necessary for defence, after the breaking of Falkenhayn's counter-attack.[1]

It is impossible in these chapters to discuss the very complicated and controversial question of the balance of fit men in England, over nineteen years of age,[2] who were available as a reinforcement for the B.E.F. before March 21, beyond those actually despatched. A figure of 150,000 is at least a conservative estimate. Haig could certainly then have been reinforced by some 175,000 fighting men (allowing for two divisions from Palestine) without any risk.

Did this omission seriously affect the ability of the British forces to resist the enemy's assault? No decided answer can be given. Haig's dispositions had proved so bad that the area most heavily attacked, that of the 5th army, had fewer troops in line and fewer reserves than any other.

[1] During April and May there were recalled from Palestine to France two complete divisions, twenty-three battalions, nine yeomanry regiments and five and a half siege batteries. The two divisions were replaced by inferior units from Mesopotamia, and the remaining battalions by driblets of native Indian troops at intervals during the summer.

[2] Boys under nineteen were not to be sent abroad, and this pledge was kept except during the great crisis (March–April 1918).

The Germans moved against this unhappy army as 5 against 1. Even if Gough had received another two or three divisions the initial break through would almost certainly have occurred exactly as it did. The tide, however, might have been stayed on the Somme. The whole speculation is really futile, for if Haig had disposed of a larger reserve, Pétain might well have been even more niggardly of immediate aid. The total number of units available on the critical days might have been precisely the same.

It has been said with plausibility and much truth that Ludendorff's admirable tactics and the faultiness of Haig's arrangements proved of immense value to the Allied cause. The enemy was drawn on to an *offensive à outrance*, which had cost him by July 750,000 irreplaceable soldiers. His splendid but inconclusive victories wore out the defensive capacity of his exhausted armies.

Similarly the disorganised retreat of the 5th army threw for the first time since August 1914 an instant and terrible light upon the great military defect of the Alliance in hours of crisis, the lack of a unified command. Pétain, it is true, had done more than he had bargained in the despatch of French troops. But by the evening of March 24 the gap in the south was widening. More ominous still, it was widening because of a deliberate divergence between the intentions of the two commanders. The British edged north-west, in order to cover the Channel ports against an eventual flanking attack. Pétain was preoccupied with the safety of Paris. "Avant tout, maintenir solidement l'armature de l'armée française...ensuite, si possible, conserver la liaison avec les armées britanniques." Such was his order to the Northern Army Group on that day. In plain words it meant that a great avenue of rupture was being opened for the enemy's benefit.

Haig saw this and acted upon it with fine energy and unselfishness. It was mainly due to his insistence that the conference at Doullens two days later appointed Foch to co-ordinate the action of the Franco-British armies on the Western Front. Clemenceau truly declared: "C'est aujourd'hui une journée historique. Le sort de la guerre va se fixer." For from co-ordination to supreme command was but a step, and an inevitable one.

Thus it happened that the extremity of defeat itself provided the condition of victory. Haig often showed himself stubborn, narrow and impervious to argument, but he has the rare and glorious distinction of bringing about his own subordination for the common cause.

III

From the breaking of the storm until the close of the war events moved at such a headlong speed that the strategy, first of defence then of counterblow, was for the most part improvised in the office of the Generalissimo. Foch, who maintained a very small *maison militaire* of picked officers, laid his plans with rigorous secrecy; the civil authorities had often but a few hours' notice of the execution of his intentions.

Consequently the British Cabinet had the smallest opportunity, even if it had the wish, of influencing the last stages of operations. It was engaged in working out a vast plan of mechanical surprise for the unfought campaign of 1919, on which almost all hopes were centred until the close of September. Sir Henry Wilson, supplest of soldiers, who had finally in March hoisted himself into Robertson's chair as a professed exponent of Lloyd Georgian strategy, found himself so situated that his main work was to keep the B.E.F. as strong as possible to serve the undisclosed plans of his old comrade Foch. The schemes in which he engaged so heartily of creating a great inter-allied front against the enemy in European and Asiatic Russia were quite inchoate at the time of the armistice.

It is now established that the naval assault in Zeebrugge had no appreciable effect in bridling the submarine. A far more serious blow was the establishment of the great mine barrage across the North Sea, in the execution of which the Americans can claim by far the larger share.

However, the British Government, as represented by Lord Northcliffe and his fellow-workers at Crewe House, can justly maintain that by the indirect but deadly weapon of propaganda they did much to ensure that the campaign of 1918 would be final. The evidence of the German military leaders is conclusive as to the venomously disabling effect upon the moral both of soldiers and civilians of the rain of leaflets which descended by air upon the battle zone or were insinuated into every part of Germany. The brave enduring heart of the enemy had been heavily smitten by the time when the Allies

[86]

turned again after finally making good their four months' defensive battle. Before considering the importance of the sudden overthrow of Bulgaria and Turkey upon the final situation, we must ask what share in the direction of the last hundred days in France was taken by the British Commander-in-Chief. All agree—no testimony could be more emphatic and glowing than that of Foch himself—that the troops performed their arduous task of continual assault with a courage and endurance unsurpassed in our history. But did British Headquarters influence the grand strategy of this autumn?

It must first be noticed that the strategy itself was made possible only by a British invention, the tank, which we always employed on a scale far greater than the French, and the tactics of which we had almost entirely evolved.

Although the Allies had from July onwards an increasing superiority in men, which by the armistice amounted to at least 35 per cent., they could not have staged their unparalleled series of ever-widening attacks without the tank, which enabled a proportionately greater economy in the use of men, as the enemy's moral grew more and more shaken by horror at the inexorability of the new weapon. Whereas on the first day of the Somme 3000 prisoners cost 60,000 casualties, between August 8 and 10 we took 20,000 Germans at a total cost of some 18,000 men.

The method which Foch gradually evolved during this last campaign has been called by the French "l'attaque articulée". It consisted in striking suddenly at a sensitive spot, then transferring the blow rapidly to a flank, so that the whole intervening area was cast into a state of flux. The scale and geographical amplitude of these blows were gradually extended; during the climax in the last week of September four tremendous assaults were delivered on successive days on the two extremities and the centre of the line between Verdun and the sea. The object, never fully realised, was to force the enemy's evacuation of his prepared positions, then to swing round on the north and south, so as to drive his masses into Northern Belgium, and separate their communications from Aix-la-Chapelle, Luxembourg and Lorraine. The failure to turn defeat into a hopeless rout was mainly due to the heroic defence of the Argonne against the furious but clumsy American onslaught. The northern German armies were thus able to

retreat towards the Meuse instead of being forced
away from it by a rapid American advance down
the river towards Liége.

During this period Haig was far more than a
mere executant of Foch's orders. It was he who
refused after August 8 to continue hammering
against the defeated enemy in front of Amiens,
in spite of the vehement pressure of the Generalissimo. By moving the battle northward and
thus outflanking the devastated heights of the
Somme, he prepared the way for vaster projects.
It was through his representations that the
Americans staged their great converging attack upon Mezières instead of directing their
principal strength eastwards against Metz. It
may even be true that it was his confidence in
his troops, and his intuition of the enemy's
exhaustion which determined Foch to make that
autumn campaign decisive. For the latter's
original intention had merely been to prepare
the way for 1919 by disengaging certain strategic
railways threatened or cut by the enemy's line.
Haig had from the first blow inspired his
subordinates with hope of victory before the
winter. "Risks which a month ago would have
been criminal to incur ought now to be incurred

as a duty. The situation is most favourable. Let each one of us act energetically, and, without hesitation, push forward to the objective" (August 24). If, obedient to the warnings of the War Cabinet, he had refrained from that culmination of boldness, the attack on the Hindenburg line, the war must almost beyond doubt have been prolonged beyond the winter.

In the last hundred days of the war he showed a vision and a calculated resolution in taking chances worthy of a great captain. His career in the war is a curious example of how exactly the same qualities in dissimilar circumstances make both a bad and a good general.

IV

That the collapse of Germany was due to the combination of economic exhaustion with military defeat few if any would deny. Even the most obdurate Easterner will not maintain that Germany fell because her weaker brethren had successively capitulated a few weeks before the suspension of arms in the West. They gave up because it was plain that their great ally had already lost the war, and could give no tittle of aid to their own extremity. It may, however, be argued that the fall of Bulgaria, Turkey and Austria-Hungary determined the moment of the German surrender, that these shocks of disruption broke the will to resistance, which might otherwise have lasted through the winter, and made necessary another campaign against the line of the Meuse. It is certainly true that the coincidence of the Bulgarian armistice with the rupture of the Hindenburg line threw Ludendorff off his balance on September 29. It was this culmination of bad news which induced him to send to Berlin the peremptory demand for an immediate armistice. But even so, it must be remembered that

(i) Great Britain had consistently opposed the Salonika expedition, had several times vainly demanded its withdrawal, and had acquiesced most reluctantly in the decision to take the final offensive. It is further believed that Milne had full discretion from Lloyd George to refuse British participation therein, if he judged fit. The role of the Salonika army, therefore, whatever its importance, was due to the attitude of the French. But for them it would not have existed in September 1918.

[91]

(ii) While the Bulgarian collapse doubtless convinced General Headquarters that the Central Alliance was falling rapidly to pieces, the demand for an *immediate armistice within twenty-four hours* was dictated by the fear of a break through in the West. Ludendorff in fact believed in the possibility of an imminent catastrophe in the West, which would have ruined his army beyond hope. Doubtless he miscalculated, and realised his miscalculation too late, when the interchange of notes with Wilson had begun.

It is therefore possible to argue that if Bulgaria had not capitulated at that moment Ludendorff would not have lost his head and underestimated the power of resistance yet left in his army. In that case he might have brought it back to the Antwerp-Meuse line, and waited on events until 1919. It is not probable but it is possible.

But it seems idle to argue that the only one of the three subsidiary triumphs for which Great Britain was responsible, the overthrow of Turkey, had any effect on the duration of the war.

Firstly, the victory of Megiddo did not precede but followed the Bulgarian collapse which had broken the spirit of General Headquarters on September 29. Secondly, the Turkish army in

Palestine contained less than a division in all of German troops; there had not therefore been any such diversion of men from the West as to affect the situation there. Thirdly, the surrender of Bulgaria provided the Allies with a new front of attack against the Central Powers; the French were on the Danube before the end of October and menacing distracted and rebellious Hungary. It also brought Rumania into direct touch with the Allied armies and gave good hope that the vital oil supplies from there would be speedily cut off. Turkey did not surrender till October 30, and her territory could obviously not be used as an immediate base of operations against the enemy such as was available from Serbia, or still more vital and imminent from Tyrol, after the Austrian Empire had collapsed. The exit of Turkey did not hasten the date of the German armistice by an hour. It was merely another proof that the weaker members of the Alliance had been kept together only by the belief that Germany would win, and thereby ensure them part at least of the gains which they had entered the war to secure.

Chapter V

CONCLUSION

ALTHOUGH the war was won as the direct consequence of an unexampled series of land battles, it is profoundly true that this result was attained only through the conduct of the war at sea. It is impossible and futile to speculate as to the ultimate issue if British sea-power had not been aimed at the economic strangulation of the Central Powers. But just because this tremendous engine of power was directed almost entirely by Great Britain no detailed account of it would be appropriate or even possible in these chapters. To deal with it adequately would require a consideration of the whole course of naval operation. Even in the Mediterranean, a subordinate theatre, though the command was exercised by a French admiral, the British contingent was generally the most important and certainly the most efficient. The closing of the Adriatic was mainly due to the cordon of British drifters, the mine barrage across the Strait of Otranto was mainly due to British effort, the convoying of merchantmen and transports through that infested region was mainly done by British ships.

It would be a mistake to suppose that our naval strategy was the carrying out of a scheme already elaborated in peace-time. It was rather the gradual improvisation of a policy made natural by the geographical conditions of self-defence.

The Navy had to protect the islands from invasion, keep the high seas free for our trade, and prevent interference with the transport of troops to France or elsewhere. To do these things it could not under modern conditions either maintain a close blockade, or bring the enemy's fleet to battle at will.

It was therefore compelled to exercise a distant or strategic blockade. This involved such a disposition of our fleet as firstly to deny the enemy access to the ocean either by way of the Channel or by the Norwegian route; secondly, to endanger his fleet movements in the northern or western area of the North Sea, by so arranging our bases that he would run the gravest risk of being cut off from a return by the convergence of superior forces upon his flanks and rear.

[95]

CONCLUSION

As soon as the British concentration had been effected and made secure (and its insecurity for the first few months of the war was never penetrated by the German Command), it naturally created the conditions for a long war. It would not necessarily have done so, but for the temperament of the Commander-in-Chief, Jellicoe, whose caution based on an exact calculation of risks was fully known to the Admiralty, when they ordered him to hoist his flag at the outbreak of war.

Jellicoe was guided throughout by the knowledge that a decisive defeat of the Grand Fleet would involve the speedy and inevitable destruction of the whole Entente. His responsibility was therefore greater, far greater, than that of any other single man on either side. On the other hand, it was a matter for speculation whether a decisive defeat of the German High Seas Fleet would involve the downfall of the Central Powers. The issue of action being so disparate, he firmly refused to engage the enemy in battle except in circumstances of his own choice, or deliberate acceptance. Why provoke the supreme hazard of a great naval battle, when it was generally accepted that time was on the side of the Entente?

[96]

CONCLUSION

It is true that this argument did not appeal to Russia. Russia was cut off from the Allies except at a few scattered points of eccentric contact, Archangel, Kola and Vladivostok; the enemy controlled the Baltic, and a long war progressively increased the danger of revolution. It was therefore natural that Russian opinion was hostile to Jellicoe's waiting policy, demanded the forcing of the Baltic, and was bitterly disappointed at the negative results of the battle of Jutland. Yet, as the event proved, it was wiser to risk the defection of Russia than to seek at all hazards a decisive battle in the North Sea to help a cruelly stricken ally.

The right policy of naval assistance to her was that pursued in 1915 with such fumbling and palsied uncertainty in the Dardanelles, where the prize was great, and the loss of the obsolete units employed unimportant to our superiority in the vital theatre. The Russians, moreover, might reasonably consider that such an effort was owing to them. For at the time it was generally believed that the escape of the *Goeben* and *Breslau* had brought Turkey into the war; and for that escape the combined mismanagement of the British Admiralty and the British admiral had been responsible. Even now, even in the light of the secret engagement already signed with Germany on August 1, it is possible to argue that Turkey would have evaded its fulfilment after the Marne, but for the presence of the two vessels in the Golden Horn, at once a proof and a threat of Germany's power.

In another way also the British concentration suggested a long draft on time for the exhaustion of the enemy. As the British islands presented a great breakwater barring egress from the North Sea except at its extremities, so they could be used no less powerfully to forbid ingress to the rest of the world. An economic blockade had been no part of our pre-war strategy. It was not of course a novel idea, for it drew its precedents from the Napoleonic struggle. But no definite conclusions had been worked out as to whether it would be either technically or diplomatically possible a century later. The Navy made it technically possible by a vast system of improvisation, which utilised every kind of craft from liners to trawlers and motor launches. The Foreign Office and the War Trade Department made it diplomatically possible by the skilful stages through which America and the other

[98]

neutrals were gradually inured to the successive evasions and contraventions of international custom and law which the participation of the chief protester, America herself, finally reduced to a complete system.

The history of the blockade is the best example in the war of the harmonious co-operation between force, diplomacy and expert knowledge, each holding the hands of the others and marching abreast. Yet even so it is improbable that Great Britain could have persevered in such a course without the risk from America of complications fatal to its attainment had not the German submarine campaign been launched. It is useless to argue whether there is any valid ethical distinction between an attempt to starve a nation by intercepting its supplies on the sea, or by sinking its cargo boats and those of neutrals by torpedo or shell. What is perfectly certain is that neutrals react very differently to the two methods. A blockade which operated through patrol and examination endangered no neutral lives, and did not entail the immediate and spectacular slaughter of enemy non-combatants.

Apart, therefore, from any question of moral guilt the German naval policy was psycho-

7-2

logically bad, and not only failed in its aim, but actually helped the British blockade to attain a completeness otherwise unrealisable.

It is well to remember that in modern war psychological appreciation of the most effective means of influencing neutrals, breaking the will of enemies and sustaining the hearts at home is a kind of indirect strategy, which may prove in the long run more effective than plans of the General Staff and all the weapons of war.

Since 1918 the Germans have repeatedly witnessed with ingenuous surprise and candid self-humiliation to their immense inferiority in these respects to the Entente peoples and in particular to the British. This is not the place to discuss whether the unexampled and frenzied efforts of their governors to remedy this defect are likely to prove successful either at home or abroad, in the event of a similar ordeal.

For EU product safety concerns, contact us at Calle de José Abascal, 56–1°,
28003 Madrid, Spain or eugpsr@cambridge.org.

www.ingramcontent.com/pod-product-compliance
Ingram Content Group UK Ltd.
Pitfield, Milton Keynes, MK11 3LW, UK
UKHW040616240426
470322UK00010B/143